Thoreau's Chair

POEMS by AARON SILVERBERG

Thoreau's Chair

POEMS by AARON SILVERBERG

For Scott,
Enjoyed sharing poetry with
you. May these soothe your way.
With lovingkindness,
Aaron

OFF THE MAP ENTERPRISES

Seattle 2001

Off The Map Enterprises, Seattle, WA

First Edition

Library of Congress Cataloging-in-Publication Data
ISBN 0-615-11962-X

Produced by Griggs Irving
Cover and interior design by Crista Goddard
Proofed by Ellen Blackstone
Cover photo by Herb Quick
Inside photo by Author (Aaron Silverberg)

Printed and bound in the United States of America.

FOR MY LOVED ONES
Joel Andreas, Marilyn, Mike, Penelope,
Bari and David

TO MY TEACHERS
Gary Snyder, Rumi, Walt Whitman, Buddha

TO TIMELESS PLACES OF BEAUTY
Breitenbush River, Bear Park, Second Beach,
Cape Sebastian, Black Pine Lake, Na Pali
may your treasures be forever savored...

TABLE OF CONTENTS

FOREWORD

Henry David Thoreau was appreciative, and sparing, of
his friends. We have on his own authority that he did
have a chair, a simple wooden one beside his own, in his
one-room cabin in Massachusetts. It is a wonderful and
telling symbol of his social yet independent mind. One
suspects that it served his imagination better empty than
when occupied, a kind of bait for his conversational spirit,
though occasionally it materialized a woodcutter, fisherman
or fellow philosopher. It was certainly an uncommon trail
from town to his cabin.

A chair like Thoreau's would be more a discovery for
Aaron Silverberg, than an invention. I can easily imagine
him casting up on the shore of Walden Pond at the end of
an afternoon blissfully lost, seized by superlatives over its
beauty, loudly proclaiming it all to the trout, water, and
woodchucks. Finding the cabin, he would have seen at
once the meaning of the chair and taken it as graciously
and enthusiastically as he would have shared the
philosopher's griddle cake and apple.

Thoreau would have been both outraged and charmed
by this flying man, this fool for love, this uncontainable
spirit. He would have loved him, as I have loved him
as a friend these many years, for his unmistakable
courage, his too-much-life-to-be-lived-all-at-oncedness,
his wild divinity.

Sometimes the gods deliver their gifts in person; more
often they send us madmen and watch us from the
clouds. The laughter and protests booming over the lake
in the dark would have pleased them, the precious candles

spent one after the other, the bread shared until it was gone. In the morning Thoreau would have dug another apple from his hoard for his guest's trail, knowing full well it would be fed to chipmunks. Such service do the gods demand of us, if we would have them visit us again.

Reader, I commend these poems to you. In them you will find passion, humor, brilliance, freedom, insight, love, and a sacred irreverence.

There is no evidence that Thoreau possessed a translation of the Sufi poet Rumi, but he would have recognized the face of the Friend.

May you recognize it as well.

Mike Price
Twisp, Washington

Thoreau's Chair

POEMS by AARON SILVERBERG

Is the one I love everywhere?

~Rumi

NO MISSING

I must find you
in the quiet
of a beckoning silence

even at the risk of
missing you completely.

Like the opaque velvet
enclosing a star
your dark smile knows
that my flickering ray
can find no other.

UNDER THIS SKIN

Under these clothes
yearns a tender offering,
a soft skin that breathes spasmodically
through hands and face, hair and ears.

Under these clothes
dances a
longing caressed
by the dimensions
of bare madrona.

Under these clothes
drifts a
meandering kiss,
tongue-fulls of
devotion
dribbling down
emancipated roots.

Under this skin is *another*,
uncontainable,
iridescent splendor.

BURNING

The fire is undulating inside you.
Open doors,
let it out.
Don't sit in the smoke and feign darkness,
lose direction.
Let the fire burn clearly.
Open doors,
clear a path,
let it light your journey.

How do stars burn in a vacuum?
How do you burn?
Such immense spaces to burn in...

What is it burning up?
What is it burning through?
Burning in the nothingness.
Burning for you.

Ripping ourselves open,
there is only the burning.
I am burning for you.
The Beloved is burning.

Beyond the open doors
will you burn with me?

Brilliantly burning,
with no yearning
for containment.

LOVE ON THE AFRICAN PLAIN

Shook open
a rare steak
wholly enjoyed
morsel by morsel.

Succulent juices on her tongue
your soul in her mouth.

A leopardess glances up
at the morning light
pouring over the Serengeti.

ODE TO THE 'SHROOM

We eat the wild mushroom to praise
the dark cellars of nature's glory,
the bright places where mycelium and roots
make love.

We eat the fungi to taste our love for the forest,
to swallow our thankfulness for the mycorrhiza.

Rotting trees take their long memories to earth.
The mushroom is the remembrance!

We kneel down to rejoice
the taking up of life
the tender from the barked.

The mystery flower returns us
to our woody woolly selves.

A HAND UP

There's no time to wait.
Hearts are reaching out!

Can't you feel the
seeking vines tickle?

Let them wrap around you.
Give them an anchor,
a hand up
toward wherever they're growing.

APOPLEXY

(where have I seen you before
loosened face bright shining eyes
dancing like feathers falling?)

near the black crows
a proud man stands

stock still

empty cap extended
(in front of a hat store.)

'cross the street a
drunken warrior

staggers

in a doorway of tears.

WILD SKAGIT
(for Robert Sund)

solemn dripping in bare trees

swollen river
foaming and cursing

mad as Ophelia's hair

green witness occasionally bowing
to the silvered court

love and sadness commingled
under
the veiled moon's moan.

BLOODBERRIES

Oregon Grape
is its official name
swollen blueberry blue   confounds.
Bitter in the mouth
the disappointment must be spat out.

To my jungle boy they are *bloodberries*
pricked and smeared bright red
gore to be relished.

Along the swaths are
the real martyrs, blackberries
where blood and sugar are sure to be mixed
growing as innocently as marriage
lavender flowers dull green beads.

Trembling for the sweetness cloak
anything not to lie in my own blood
waiting for you
in an abandoned bush.

Oregon Grape
is its official name.
Bitter in the mouth
the disappointment must be spat out.

THE END OF APATHY

Don't be deceived by
lizard-skin comforts or
patent leather charm.
Aim for a destination
that *you* fashion.

Stop standing in cash machine lines
waiting for your lover
to be neatly spat out.
Make your life a great
protest cause and
demonstrate regularly!

Notice what you choose and
keep choosing it
over and over again.
That's how mountainsides become forests!

Deepen your practice by
being the practice.
Leave the questions and doubts
to talk-show hosts.

Don't be shy about loving yourself.
Lions lie on the savannah in ecstasy.
When you have too much, bear fruit!
Feed as many as you can.

Passion is contagious. Spread it!
Don't stand on ceremony,
reach out and caress it.
Relentless loving is the only way in!

NEOLITHIC SUNRISE

Distant flock...
long black sideways smoke.
Grunts and snorts
would be sweet music.
Rotting meat smells strong.

Sharpening point
keeps chill off hands.
Looking for sign.
Has brush been trampled?
Kicking dung, how old?
Listening to ground.
No drumming, no food.

Hyena laugh like wet woman and
slink around behind.
Spear-throwers draw pictures in
wet sand.

Spinning fire stick
makes nose wrinkle.
New fire is good.
Bone and gristle
pop and sizzle.
Hot meat is greasy and
warms the throat.

Will the wind carry good smell?

Where is moon in sky?

Women pluck herb and berry.
Eagle screams in sky.
Waiting.
We must rest breath for quick chase.

What do grasshoppers say?
Meelop finds turtle eggs.
Even crows are restless
and moving quickly.

Is Hashun's magic fading?
Plenty fish but we need many fur skins for
winter cave.
Many bones in sky.
Caribou and wolf dance in secret.
My point would like to dance with them.

Grass and reeds are good and dry for
fire and tying points.

The long shadow spears say to go
deeper and faster and quieter into the wood.
Fat beaver are not so quick into water.

Come! We must have hot blood or
the song of hollow trees will take spirit.

THE DEATH OF THE MUSHROOM GODDESS

At the meadow's edge, where the forest leans
and the blood of cedars drips down

a young fawn hesitates.

Black nose twitching at mid-air
scent of the mushroom goddess,
her tumbled basket a jumbled orgy
of rife fungi.

Her creased hands caress smooth fruit
spent penises fresh from the cavorting
the fragrant trail of her departed lover.
Offerings of musky Orpheus from the underworld.

Tenderly lifting each wrinkle
skirting white underbelly
unbuttoning the honeycomb.
The muted accordion of tangoed youth.

Inhaling boletus in long draughts
mourning the torn belly into hers
belaying the slender stem with barked fingertips.
She climbs up and in.

Her womb remembers the pressing
lidless eye of a hurricane.

The sweat-laced bull nosing past
a frenzied flutter of red brocade.

Reaching out over the slow race of her universe
she grabs both horns.
Shuddering under the lovesword stab
sliding into the Great Beast
she lies still.

The sun cries through the old man's beard.
The fawn licks the triumph pooling beneath her eyes.

OLD MAN CEDAR

Patient in the forest
and forgiving.
His red-purple skin
full of passion.
His gray-green dusting of
wisdom waiting, waiting
for the two-legged to ask
for more skin.

And though he loves the sky
and the wind,
he lies down,
makes a canoe and clothes
for his shivering brother.

Old Man Cedar is noble and red
through and through.

When the two-legged is done
running and singing in the sweet forest,
Old Man Cedar will take back his blood
and stand tall again.

SMOKY SUNRISE OVER SUMMIT LAKE

sheet of goose/duck/insect flecks
crossing still water

upside down tree-line jiggling
like new-born jello

ghost mountains curving up
out of horizon like
a lover slowly rising

a lone canoe kisses water

hush

it is here

LOVINGKINDNESS

Imagine a world where everything is alive
and nothing is dead.

Imagine the beauty you find in the things around you
comes from their mutual love and regard.

Imagine the rising and falling of your every breath
is the breath of the entire planet, the entire universe.

Imagine there is nothing to possess and nothing that
can possess you.

Imagine you can gently stop looking for that love out
there,
and simply invite it in.

Go ahead, invite it in.

WILD SKINS

dead ahead
not three paces
two mule deer
females
5 feet plus

50-lb. packs creak
twitching noses
furrythick ears
liquid brown eyes
large enough to drown in

no possessions
quickened hearts exchange

hooves prancing closer
gamey smell devours
our knowing

shutters click
and they're gone

soon at the trailhead
we lean our packs against the car
and shed our wild skins.

THOREAU'S CHAIR

Chocolate-brown maple and slightly askew
it sits empty
or so it seems
to the casual viewer.

Only one today,
on others
there are two for friendship or
three for society.

A peculiar light provides
patient reflection of what's there.

This is where the creator sits,
resting amid the songs and stories
of common folk.

Henry David came upon the wood
to confront what persisted
to befriend what subsisted.

I reserve his chair for you, beloved reader,
perpetual gift to the Guest that visits,
that wanders monkishly bemused.

Sit a spell in it, bedazzled.

WHERE THE ANT GOES

Do you remember how hard it was
to crush an ant?

You would press your finger
with all your might and backing off
slowly discover a miracle of movement.

Your heart would do a backflip and
bending down, unsure how to
kiss the microscopic steel-clamped jaws,
you would press onward
your force of death undoing the miracle.

But when the ant was vanquished for good
you wanted to follow its tiny soul
backward/forward/sideways
however it made its way to the place
you cannot press
cannot touch
cannot hold tenderly in your troubled hand.

WINGED SURVIVOR

Under the cover of night
I flew back
to a thin new forestry.

I had given up my two awkward legs
in a cold drawer
of shiny stainless steel.

No one stopped to sniff and eat me.

As they examined the carcass for clues
I poked in my feathers
for a familiar scent.

The stringy feel of cedar is good
under my talons' flex
but my eyes droop open and close
as I remember
the death screams and agony
of a human
who could not hear
the death screams and agony
of so many creatures
that had fallen before.

AGITATION

I used to laugh at birds
their endless agitation.

I no longer do
since they looked back at mine.

TAHOMA DANCE

Crack the window
while you sleep

                    out you'll blow

through the garden
over neighbors' trees
street lights   power lines   highways waterfall

where ducks float like loaves.

Skirting scree and fir
uncondensed milk
spiraling upward.

Needles for breath
glaciered hands kneading rock into soil
frigid waters peeing
wizened seed.
Nestling with
lupine   paintbrush   bluebells.

Curlicuing mist.

Gaia's blind caress.

A tantric beggar
buried in bliss.

ENCORE

There are no rules
governing who we love.

Capricious,
the wind lifts waves
into dancing whitecaps.

Bone teacups teetering
in china saucers,
love's fragile choosing.

We look into each other
two threads of starlight
kissing silently
across the long night.

A flamelick cannot cease
its tender raging.

Quenched by cuddling
children break it,
unafraid of the play.

Naked we laugh!
So many curtains have fallen,
the players walking out
joining hands for a bow.

ALREADY ARRIVED

My son Joel and I went to the nearby park together.
I sat at the far end of the children's wooden play tower,
basking in the dusking sun.
Joel played nearby, all around me, and finally went off
by himself to swing on the swings.

A part of me wanted to watch over him and assure his
safety. Another part knew better and I stayed to enjoy my
own sustained peace.

When I went over to join him, he walked up to me and
said, "Let's go home Dad."
I replied, "What a wonderful idea."

As we strolled down the path I held his hand, but almost
immediately he moved my hand around his shoulder and
hugged my thigh.
We walked in this awkwardly beautiful manner down
toward the basketball court.

He said to me, "Dad, I love you so much."
With a tear in my eye, I replied,
"I love you too Joey, so much."

It was a little embarrasing. The court was full of strong,
sweaty, bare-chested young men. But I didn't let go until
the very last second.

On the other side of the court he ran up ahead.
I watched his sturdy little frame pad up the blacktop
wishing with all my might that this precious little boy

never change or
that I might never reach the turnoff
head between two tall firs,
getting somewhere
when I had already arrived.

DIVERSIONS

if only life were linear
like one of those ultra-modern sidewalks
at the airport.

but there are always diversions
the ads along the way or
you run into a friend you haven't seen in years or
you forgot to pack something or
you get hungry and decide to snack or
you get to thinking about how much you'd rather
be home with your children or lover or garden or ...

until
you can't remember where you were headed or
what flight would get you there.

all of us really know where conveyor belts lead...
coffins into crematoriums,
Batman to his 700th doom.

nothing more precious can happen than the thing
breaking down.

when you can hop off
walk   dance   sing   dawdle
in your own sweet time.

YOUR LIFE IS DRAMATIC

Every office worker is waiting
without a breath
for that swashbuckling pirate
dagger clenched in sourgnashed teeth
to swing through the sterile
plate glass window
to rape and plunder the computer and
its archfiend monitor, while the mouse scurries for cover,
to yell at the top of his east end'r lungs
"Grab the rope, matey, and swing yer arse outta here!"

And thence to sail to some Caribbean island where
bare-breasted women and children move like waves.

There is that one peculiar moment of terror
when the office worker grabs the proffered twine
releasing a breath held for years
only to choke on the next
while the shards of mangled glass
gleam with sharkly delight.

The office worker is repelled and strangely attracted
by the noxious pirate
whose mouth is moving
without sound
as the coarse rope swings out
through the sickening maw.

The office worker jolts awake
from a monoxide slumber.

ashen . . . aghast
Peering through the strained driplets.

Wondering, wondering, wondering
where the drama of a lifetime goes
when it is not played out.

IT'S ALL IN THE EYES

It was a Greyhound bus
with those big, overstuffed seats.

Thirty-something kids piled into it
through the diesel exhaust
and it rumbled southward
from Chicago to Springfield.
The Eighth Grade Field Trip.

Grant's tomb
Lincoln's log cabin
The radio blared "Let it be"
while we sang the theme song to
Gilligan's Island at the top of our lungs.
Reese's peanut butter cups clung to the roof of my mouth.

Nonchalantly chucking popcorn
across the aisle.
Delighted when the errant kernel
landed down the back of a shirt or
better yet
stuck in the front of a blouse.

Someone rolled toilet paper down the aisle.
Mike smeared on Diane's lipstick
and kissed as many windows as he could.

A historic stop at the tourist shop in New Salem.
A sea of alpine felt hats with huge white feathers
bobbed up and down.

Even Nancy wore one of those green monstrosities.
I wanted to sing something from "The Sound of Music."
Maybe it would've even gotten a laugh or two.

It got dark on the way back and everyone pulled down
the window shades and pressed the buttons of the
overhead reading lights on and off
on and off.

I can't remember who started the staring contests but
it was a natural excuse to get Nancy onto my lap.
We went for it eyeball-to-eyeball.

She had the most beautiful face I'd ever seen.
Her eyes were as brown as the liquid center of a tootsie pop.

When her irises danced back and forth across mine
I felt jolts of joy in my heart.

After graduation I didn't see her until I was 17.
Nancy and her friend just stood there looking up at me in
amazement, "Wow, you sure have *grown*!"
            "Boy have you *changed*!"

I was flattered but Nancy had gotten acne too,
and no one knew what to say.
They shuffled off to the elevator and out of my life.
I imagine she's out there somewhere in the suburbs
with a couple of teenagers driving a new-smelling car and
trying to keep it all together.

Sometimes late at night
the light of her face wakes me up
and I lie there and let it shine all over me.

MORNING AIKIDO

deep breath
in unison
resounding clack!

the one body of many
hissing
into the rafters -- arises!

cool wood on bare feet
muffled thumps
silent spinning bodies
tumble and tumble and tumble
across the floor

stiff gis yield
to warm, round bellies.

straight lines bend.

the long hall is cut
into circles
snapped out
into delicate origami.

just outside
the breath still steams...

On-nee-gosh-e-mas!
let's play.

LIFE AS A BODY

Lay the body down.
Pick the body up.
Touch another body.
Wash/feed/clothe the body.
Listen to the body's pain.
Decide what to do with the body.
Rest the body.
Acknowledge you even have a body.
Look at skeletons in a museum and shiver.
Forgive the mind.
Walk the body.
Laugh the body.
Dance in a larger body.
Soak the body.
Float the body.
Soothe the body.
Search out the body electric.
Bring home the body.
Give up the body.
Admire other bodies.
Want particular bodies.
Push the body past its limits.
Ignore the body.
Heal broken parts of the body.
Feel alone in the body.
Fearfully refuse to ask on the body's behalf.
Allow others the enjoyment of this body.
Fail to find compassion for older bodies.
Watch the body change.
Long for a different body.
Judge the body.

Laugh at other bodies.
Make do with this body.
Leave the body

WHAT IF

what if
> you would take the gun from your head
> gently uncock the trigger
> and set it down?

what if
> you were to let the job go by
> and spend your days
> in a small holy place
> remembering you are a piece of perfection
> a cherished handiwork of the Beloved?

what if
> you dwelled with God
> while your heart was still beating
> unafraid to love your life completely
> like the newborn you are every day
> every precious page of suffering
> a delight for the swollen lover
> behind those eyes?

what if
> this never-ending tenderness,
> your only inheritance
> was all you passed on?

what if

PROSPERITY

several hours outdoors daily,
moving freely,
juicy conversations,
tears of happiness,
a good mess,
animal sounds,
a nap,
a hand-written letter,
chance encounter,
candlelight at night,
subtle aromatics,
singing in the shower,
watching children play,
gazing at an entire sunset,
inventing constellations,
helping someone in person,
listening,
a sacred place alone,
wind on bare skin,
giving what others can receive,
receiving what others give,
remembered dreams,
staying in bed,
certainly home.

I LIKE

i like
the ooze of your caramel eyes.
i like
the heat lightning crossing your face in flashes.
i like
your hips' jangle with mine a few feet away.
i like
crawling through the rasp 'n' razz
of your voice's jazz joint.
i like
your wild-ass temper, kicking like a semi's backdraft.
i like
your gentle friendship.
i like
crying with you, sobbing down dams of hurt.
i like
your face, the exquisite tip of your nose.
i like
being quiet with you, nestled in slivers of morning light.
i like
the way my body and soul are your home.
i like
dipping this pen in my heart,
writing you what's true and lovely and enduring.

NO WORDS

Across from one another we lie
legs entwined
faces lit with holy magic.

There in the candlelit bed
in the middle of the quiet night
gazing gently into each other
no words.

Two faces flickering with the radiance of love.

AT THE TONE, THE TIME WILL BE NOW

Today I want to fast
to feast upon you
to drink from your eyes
to eat precious morsels
from your fingertips
to bathe in your light
to rest my skin upon yours
in yours
besides yours.
Closing my eyes I
thrill
to the love-honey pouring through
your voice.

I am yours
naked smile
rocking prayer of sighs
brilliant thrust of a jellyfish
billowing.

IMPERMANENCE

Deep in my wormwood smile
your body thrums
to purple raindrops.

Each dancer recoils lightly
from the rainbow's edge.

You rise and fall on my passion
till the marrow sings.

Nothing remains the same in
Buddha's orgy.

WOMAN

cherry blossom
        ruffled in evening's breeze

concern
        about her impossibly soft petals

determination
        to fix her fruit and
        pass on her sweetness

terror
        when the trunk is not
        well barked

happy
        to waft scent alluring

obsessed
        with color and
        being noticed

empowered
        in a symphony of blossoms

in love
        with the sun, the shade and
        the morning dew

faithful
        to the earth, to the mouth
        partaking her succulence

joyful
        in the succession of bloom.

IN A PUFF OF SMOKE

my love for you is not the flame
the unblinking eye
seeking out a prisoner
the lustrous wanting
the shameless search.

no, my love is the flickering
extinguished.
the snuffed-candle moment
when the Beloved closes on itself
with infinite satisfaction.

WELL SPENT

There's a wild touch
in your eyes
that I keep reaching for,
a wild river
that keeps coursing
through my heart.

I can't stop looking at you
looking for you
looking inside/out
emptying myself to make
more room for you.

Unmake the bed I've kept
too neatly.
Wreck this life
of bankrolled breath.

Leave me like the
ebbed beachside
strewn with passion well spent.

THIRTEEN PINTS

How tiring withholding holy blood in this
meager sack.
What flattery to believe it does less good
elsewhere.

Gazing around I see the rich barter of life.

I wait impatiently to redeem these thirteen pints
and nothing meets my price!

Give away your self-importance.
Leave it at the coat-check and toss the claim token.

Go hunting prepared for both outcomes.
Swap your cowardice
for the boldness of a wild animal.
Awaken to a sudden chance!

THE REFUGEE'S TRAIL

Do you have a matador's cape
An offering for the raging bull
of your thoughts' charge?

Are you glistening in the matador's finery?
Are the dramatic horns of conquest
echoing in your chest?
Without the bull, are you lonely, perhaps terrified
as your radiant sword stabs through nothing but
imagined sinew?

What if you were to walk
past the coliseum
this morning?
Out into the blazing Toledo sunshine
the Quixotian plain
where a man is but a few indentations in sandy dirt
a few puffs of water vapor.

Is there any glory without seething rage?

Peaceful feet answer, one courageous footfall after another.

AMAZING

I may not get it right.
I certainly won't decide rationally
following my wild river
through chasms of whitewater
clear-pouring pitchers of affection
dangling in rubber-tube loiter.

I certainly will love outrageously
beyond the ken of those upriver.
I will be irritating to some,
currents unpredictable,
passions capricious,
yet some will pursue this intrigue.

Cast off in this paltry canoe.
Feel the amazement of its bark.
Dip this paddle into the patient water
over and over,
beaded driplets hanging on
at the astonishing return.

LOVETREMBLES

A tree never stops trembling in the wind
but it still stays there.

The wind asks for forgiveness everywhere
searching   blowing
through thin hair on babies' heads
through silver hairs on aged toes
kissing all it can.

Can you kiss your deepest fears?
Can you treasure your constant trembling?

Climb the aspen and sit.
Listen to the sounds of golden shivers.

Make your peace now.

DWELLING

When the day ends
who do you know?

How many times did you gaze
into trusting eyes?

How much of your sweet sweet time
did you spend hiding out?

How long can you breathe with that reed
from under the pond?

When did you last hear an elk's bugle, winds
whip through mountaintops or gaze upon a
tai-chi fog dancing?

Go where your god takes you
beyond the valleys of good and evil
where your dancing leaves no questions and
your singing no answers.

INSIDE AURA

Come with me on a
journey inward
to the Beloved's chambers.

Buddha's smile will be our loveseat.

A generous garden
we will grow
wild and lovely
entwined and entwining

wearing only the morning's glow.

IF TODAY

if today
I fell like a ripe pear
bruised and sweet and
begged earth open.

if today
my prayer flag ripped and tattered
scattered across the Tibetan plain.

if today
my eyes stayed inward
bathed in brilliant light.

if today
I stepped off cliffs
slid deep into lagoons
frothed upward through raging rivers.

if today
I crumbled in microscopic bits
cascading down desert dunes.

if today
I migrated across crystal blue fields with
ruby wings.

if today
I quelled my quivering under the sure-footed
succulent red clover.

if today
I ambled westward past sunset with tireless white egrets.

if today
I wept freely over Kauai, Tahiti, Pele.

if today
I danced deep in Gaia's faults.

if today
I disappointed everyone except
the lapis dusk.

if today
I nestled in the shade beneath
the shade.

if today
I prayed over Everest and under Marino.

if today
I wandered through the lungs of my enemies
and kissed them from the inside.

if today
I conceded victory to the sweet tyranny of blackberry.

if today
I was all that I loved.

FORGIVENESS

There's a story that my love
got left behind
in the womb
in my father's mournful eyes
with a lover I failed to serve
with sufficient devotion.

There are a thousand tales about my imperfection
my loneliness my sorrow

There is a creation mythology for every unhappiness.

The truth is that *I* am the creator of these spoken masks.

I am terrified of my own beautiful and precious
god-presence.

Please laugh at my ridiculous exploits, love conquered,
love betrayed, love sautéed.

Love the hermit crab part of me that is not
camouflage.

I have dreamt up my own precariousness and must
awaken to this viciously guarded secret.

I am the eternal bejeweled night light that I feign seeking.
I have sought refuge from my journey in human form.
At death I will return to my infinite splendor
with you as my light-traveling companions.

What lovely nonsense this human drama has been!

We are the spiraling energy dancing forever.

the way you make love is the way God will be with you

~Rumi

NOTES:

Quote, page 1, from "The Essential Rumi," the poem "Community of Spirit," page 4.

Burning is dedicated to Rumi and Shams of Tabriz. It is about the fire that can never go out.

Love on the African Plain is really a theory, that physical and sexual "eating" are actually one partaking. How different to think of what we eat as still having life force that becomes part of our own.

Ode to the 'Shroom, is a paen to the Pacific Northwest's abundance of mushrooms, supporting our magnificent rainforests.

Apoplexy is about street life in downtown Seattle, the simultaneous loss and retention of human dignity.

Wild Skagit is about the amazing dance between sky and that great river. Great love affairs are not only between human beings.

Bloodberries is about the bitterness of divorce and the necessity of moving on.

The End of Apathy is about mature love, offering your fullness like a ripened wheat field just before harvest.

Neolithic Sunrise is my reimagination of Neolithic consciousness, the simplicity of animal life that was so powerful and immediate.

Mushroom Goddess, I dedicate to Earth mothers, who have spent their wondrous powers gathering and delighting, beneficently blessing this rich planet.

Old Man Cedar is the voice of native America, where plant and person exchange continually, living and dying for one another.

Smoky Sunrise over Summit Lake was conceived on this British Columbia lake, where I took the accompanying photo.

Wild Skins is about a backpacking trip I took in the Sourdough Mountains (Bear Park) beyond Sunrise (in Mt. Rainier National Park). Hearing elk bugle at 1AM is as riveting as it gets.

Thoreau's Chair is where I hope you find yourself more often.

Where the Ant Goes just came to me in the Seattle bus tunnel.

Winged Survivor is about metamorphosis/reincarnation and the lesson(s) that transition may contain.

Encore I dedicate to my loving sister, who found me after 40 years of never being introduced (a miracle!). Our reunion, her kids and mine, will always make me cry with joy.

It's All in the Eyes is how I came of age in Chicago. Illinois.

Morning Aikido was composed on a beautiful crisp November day on Bainbridge Island, during an Aikido retreat.

Woman I dedicate to all the women in my life. How much they have enriched me!

Thirteen Pints is the lifeblood of this humble gardener. How much I admire the nurse trees that lie down in the old growth forest and feed the tender saplings!

The Refugee's Trail is a call to my fellow men to find a work inside their hearts that is not isolating or destructive. I dedicate it to Thich Nhat Hanh, an inspiring voice of peace.

Lovetrembles was composed in the sumptuous Methow Valley fall, where the aspens coin the finest gold.

Inside Aura is my gift to all friends and lovers, especially reverently naked in the Breitenbush hot springs, gazing.

If Today is my Tibetan love poem, to the transcendence of love beyond any confines.

Forgiveness is what I pray for, from the eternal benevolent soul that we all are.

Quote, page 59, from "The Essential Rumi," the poem "Breadmaking," page 185.

ORDER INFORMATION:

Title: THOREAU'S CHAIR
U.S. Price: $12.95

Shipping: Add $5.00
Sales Tax: (WA residents only) add 8.6%

Contact:

AARON SILVERBERG
coachajs@home.com
www.offthemap.net
206.941.1878

LIBERATION COACHING

Liberation coaching is the process of freeing you from suffering and empowering you to create the life of your happiness.

The author, Aaron Silverberg, is a professionally-certified life coach. He offers liberation coaching to individuals, families, organizations and communities.

You may reach Aaron at 206.941.1878
or via email at coachajs@home.com.
Aaron's website is www.offthemap.net